GW01339386

Trombone for Kids

How to Play, Master the Basics with Slide and Brass Brilliance

© **Copyright 2024 - All rights reserved.**

The content contained within this book may not be reproduced, duplicated, or transmitted without direct written permission from the author or the publisher.

Under no circumstances will any blame or legal responsibility be held against the publisher or author for any damages, reparation, or monetary loss due to the information contained within this book, either directly or indirectly.

Legal Notice:

This book is copyright-protected. It is only for personal use. You cannot amend, distribute, sell, use, quote, or paraphrase any part of the content within this book without the consent of the author or publisher.

Disclaimer Notice:

Please note the information contained within this document is for educational and entertainment purposes only. All effort has been executed to present accurate, up-to-date, reliable, and complete information. No warranties of any kind are declared or implied. Readers acknowledge that the author is not engaging in the rendering of legal, financial, medical, or professional advice. The content within this book has been derived from various sources. Please consult a licensed professional before attempting any techniques outlined in this book.

By reading this document, the reader agrees that under no circumstances is the author responsible for any losses, direct or indirect, that are incurred as a result of the use of the information contained within this document, including, but not limited to, errors, omissions, or inaccuracies.

Table of Contents

Introduction 1

Chapter 1: Introduction to the Trombone 3

Chapter 2: Getting Started with the Trombone 11

Chapter 3: Trombone Playing Techniques 27

Chapter 4: Building Trombone Skills 37

Chapter 5: Playing Trombone Music 47

Chapter 6: Trombone Care and
Maintenance 55

Chapter 7: Exploring Trombone History
and Repertoire 61

Conclusion 67

References 69

Introduction

Are you a fan of trumpet-like instruments? Do you find the sound of the trombone fascinating? Can you feel the trombone calling to the music lover in you? Maybe you have seen different players make the instrument sound divine and thought to yourself, "I want to be like them." Well, you absolutely can! You, too, can master the skill of playing this lovely instrument; this book is here to ensure that happens.

Trombone for Kids is a book written with you in mind. It is a comprehensive guide that gives you access to the knowledge you need for an amazing trombone-playing career. This book begins with an overview of the trombone, introducing you properly to the instrument and its musical and cultural significance. Beyond that is everything from selecting the best trombone to the techniques you can use to play melodies and how to maintain your trombone's sound. Each chapter is packed with tips on how to play this amazing instrument.

Sure, there are other books about the trombone like this one, but this book stands out with its simple and clear explanations. It has lots of hands-on exercises, step-by-step guides, and well-detailed information to make you a trombone star. It doesn't matter if you are just learning your first musical instrument or already have some background knowledge of the trombone. This book will build your skills and make you more confident about playing any musical instrument.

Like with every other skill, learning to play the trombone may not always be easy; sometimes, you'll feel like the stress isn't worth it. Don't worry; all you need is a little bit of patience and dedication. You can achieve your dreams of playing trombone with great skill just like the famous players did. They don't have two heads or extra limbs on their bodies. So, buckle up and get ready for an adventure of a lifetime. Your throne in the trombone kingdom awaits you.

Chapter 1: Introduction to the Trombone

Did you know the trombone was called 'sackbut' during the 1600s? The instrument has been in existence for quite some time. Think back to when your great-grandparents were alive. Who knows? Maybe one of them or someone they knew played the instrument during their time. That's how old it is. This centuries-old instrument is still here and sounds so cool that it caught your attention. Isn't that amazing? Want to know another fun fact? The trombone was first played at a wedding! Yes, you read right. It was a wedding between royalties, the Duke of Burgundy, Charles the Bold, and Princess Margaret of England back in 1468.

1. *Did you know the trombone was called 'sackbut' during the 1600s? Source: https://unsplash.com/photos/person-playing-trumpet-in-grayscale-photography-GZJisCUR2p0*

The word 'trombone' is Italian for 'big trumpet,' and if you don't already know this, the trombone is a brass instrument. Just like a bass guitar for the family of guitars, the trombone is the one with the deep, low voice for the family of the trumpets. In every brass band, the trombone is always present with its lovely tone that adds to the music. It is an exceptional musical instrument with tones that can be surprisingly soothing. It's like a deep, comforting voice. Unlike some high-pitched instruments, there's no harshness to its sound. It can fill a room with mellow energy, perfect for setting the mood for a small gathering.

The beauty of the trombone is that it can be powerful and gentle. In the hands of a skilled player, it can bellow, adding a magic touch to musical pieces by orchestras and brass bands. Even beginners like you can create beautiful, simple melodies. The trombone's slide might look intimidating at first, but you'll get the hang of it. Think of it like an extension of your hand. It allows you to play notes easily and explore trombone-playing techniques.

You don't need many years of training with the trombone to play awesome melodies. The instrument allows you to experiment with notes at any level. Just start with the basics, and you're good to go. As you get comfortable, you can gradually pick up complicated playing skills while enjoying the sounds you produce. There's no pressure to perform perfectly or master musical pieces that famous composers can play; just focus on having fun, finding your unique style, and letting your trombone's mellow tone warm the heart of whoever is listening to you play.

The trombone is your perfect match if you're looking for an instrument that gives a relaxed vibe. It allows you to explore your love for music and lets you discover the joy of creating music, one note at a time.

Overview of the Trombone as a Wind Instrument

The trombone stands out from the crowd in the brass instrument family. First, it isn't shaped like any of the other wind instruments. The trombone is shaped like a sleek, curved metal tube that stretches out, ending in a wide, welcoming bell that makes it sound loud enough. Unlike the other members of the brass family, like the trumpet, cornet, and tuba, which use valves to produce different notes, the trombone has something called a slide. The trombone's slide is the part of the instrument used to change the pitch of the notes played by pushing and pulling it in and out.

This sliding wonder has a long and interesting history. Believe it or not, its origins go back to the 15th century – that's a whole five hundred-plus years ago! Now, that's something ancient. Back then, it wasn't called a trombone, but a funny-sounding name – a sackbut. Over time, the instrument evolved, the slide became smoother, and the sackbut transformed into the trombone you know and want to learn about today.

One of the coolest things about the trombone is that it is versatile. This means that you can play the trombone to any kind of music, and it will still sound amazing, almost like it was made for that style of music. It's a natural-born team player, usually heard amongst music bands and orchestras where it blends beautifully with violins, cellos, flutes, and other brass instruments. The trombone can play very low notes that rumble deep in your chest and surprisingly high notes that can pierce the air. It's no wonder that musicians in music bands play this instrument. This flexibility allows the trombone to play a wide range of music, from calming classical pieces to lively jazz standards.

How the Instrument Is Played

Making music with a trombone starts with a small but mighty piece called the mouthpiece. This is where you blow air into the instrument. Think about a whistle and how you must blow air into it to make that sharp sound you hear. That's kind of how it is with the trombone. The air then travels the long journey through the trombone's tube, and that's where the magic happens. The player controls the air's vibration by moving the slide in and out at just the right moment, shaping it into different musical notes. This is how you make the trombone sing.

2. The player controls the air's vibration by moving the slide in and out at just the right moment. Source: https://unsplash.com/photos/a-young-boy-playing-a-trombone-in-a-band-QhPa1rs3KDk

The slide, however, isn't just for decoration. It's the key to playing different notes. The slide has seven special positions. Each position changes the pitch of the sound that comes out. A big part of being a trombone player is learning exactly where those seven positions are on the slide. Knowing where the positions are is important, but playing the trombone also involves moving the slide quickly and smoothly between them.

The way the trombone is played, and the different sounds it can produce have made it an instrument that music bands have loved to feature for centuries. It's more than just metal and air; it's a powerful tool for musicians to express their emotions. It can boom with excitement, sing with joy, or even shout with anger. The trombone truly speaks in many voices, making it such a captivating instrument loved by many.

The Musical and Cultural Significance of the Trombone

The trombone has always been a key player in the music scene over the years. People who play the trombone are called trombonists, and for hundreds of years, they have been adding their unique sound to some of the most famous musical pieces ever written. When you listen to a grand orchestra playing a beautiful and powerful piece by famous composers like Mozart, Beethoven, or Wagner, you will hear not only the sounds of musical instruments like violins, flutes, and drums but also a deep and rich sound that fills the room and adds a touch of drama. That's the trombone. Composers loved using the trombone because it could create such a strong and exciting feeling in their music.

3. *The trombone is often a key instrument in a grand orchestra. Source: https://unsplash.com/photos/a-group-of-people-sitting-next-to-each-other-in-front-of-a-band-pseEmMT-kyo*

It wasn't always like this, though. In the olden days, trombones were mostly used in church music. They were like extra voices for the singers, helping to fill out the sound and make the music more powerful, especially for the lower parts.

This lasted until composers realized how cool the trombone sounded and how it could be used for more than just church music. They started putting it in all sorts of orchestra pieces alongside violins, flutes, and all the other instruments. This brought about a change in the trombone family, too. Originally, there were trombones of different sizes, like having a big brother, little brother, and middle brother trombone. But for orchestras, composers mostly wanted the middle brother – the tenor trombone. It was just the right size for playing all the different parts they were writing.

For the trombonists back then, playing the instrument and blending with other musicians wasn't a piece of cake. They often had to bring their own instrument, unlike other musicians who played instruments provided by their workplaces. This meant they had to be extra careful with their precious trombones, especially if they played in military bands. Also, some of these military trombones were quite big and heavy. Imagine carrying them around all day.

Luckily, things got easier for trombonists over time. Orchestras mostly used the tenor trombone, which was more practical, and composers kept writing amazing music that featured this special instrument. Sure, trombones are a key part of a marching band's sound. They are perfect for adding depth to the music, that full feeling you get when the whole band plays together. But they also bring something special to the performance you see. Marching bands often have routines with synchronized movements, and trombone players use their slides – that long part that stretches out – to be part of the show. They move them up and down in time with the music, adding another layer of excitement. It's like a built-in dance move, just for trombones.

This instrument has been around for a long time, and in different parts of the world, people have given it all sorts of interesting meanings. For example, in Christianity, the trombone has become a symbol of something truly powerful – the voice of God himself. This might seem surprising, but imagine that deep, rich sound of a trombone filling a grand cathedral. It's easy to see how people might have thought it sounded like a powerful, otherworldly voice speaking directly to them. The trombone is not just a metal pipe that sings melodies. It's an instrument with a rich history and a surprising connection to the divine.

Chapter 2: Getting Started with the Trombone

Have you seen a helicopter lift from the ground into the air? It looks pretty easy, right? Don't be fooled by how easy the movement looks. There are a whole lot of mechanisms that come together to make that happen. Importantly, a pilot has learned how to work with the mechanisms to make the helicopter fly. As you know, nobody came out of their mother's tummy already as a pilot with aviator glasses. They all went through training to become one.

4. *Learning how to play the trombone takes practice and patience. Source: https://www.flickr.com/photos/slgc/6763174275*

Learning to fly a helicopter is not an easy task. It requires lots of time, patience, dedication, and, more importantly, focus. You cannot be flying a helicopter while chit-chatting or watching a football game. You probably know how that would end already. The number of controls and buttons on the copter can make you dizzy, and you would have to understand better how each element works for the copter to fly smoothly.

Luckily for you, the trombone isn't as difficult as the helicopter. However, like with the helicopter, you must learn about the basic parts of the trombone so you can make it sing smoothly. It doesn't have too many mechanisms like the helicopter, but you still need to be patient and dedicated to mastering it. Compared to the helicopter's controls, the trombone has a slide - a single mechanism with a big effect. Your job is to learn how to position your lips and blow the right amount of air to produce a clear sound. You must also practice holding the instrument with the right-hand positioning and posture to avoid strain in any part of your body.

As a beginner, this is a new journey for you, but don't worry. You have this guide for the rest of your trombone training days. This chapter will first teach you how to select the best trombone that works for you. This is important because there are different types of trombones, and you might like one more than the others. That is where it all begins.

Next, you will be introduced to the different parts of the trombone. Learning about the parts of the trombone will help you understand the instrument better and make you appreciate it even more. For instance, the pilots must first learn which button does what before they can practice flying the helicopter. This is important because if they mix up the controls and tap one button they are not supposed to, the result could be disastrous. You don't want to experience that with your trombone.

Lastly, you will be guided through the proper ways to position your hands and body posture while playing your beloved instrument. Hand positioning and posture are foundational knowledge you need as a beginner. If you miss it now, you might end up playing good notes but with a bad posture; this may lead to injuries and strain in your body. It's best to avoid that now that you are just starting. Get your book and pen. It's time for your first trombone class.

Selecting the Right Trombone and Equipment

The very first step to playing the trombone is selecting the one suitable for you. However, since you don't know much about the instrument, it might be difficult to decide. Below are some tips and key things to consider when searching for your new friend:

1. **What type of trombone to get**? There are several types of trombones to select from. Here are some of them:

    a. **Soprano Trombone**: The soprano trombone is like a tiny trumpet. It is the smallest of the trombone family and is nicknamed slide trumpet. It is designed to produce some of the highest notes and because of its high-pitched voice, it is sometimes used to replace a trumpet in a music band. It sounds great, but finding and learning to play it can be challenging because it is not very popular.

5. *Soprano Trombone. Source: Jonathan Harker, CC BY 4.0 <https://creativecommons.org/licenses/by/4.0>, via Wikimedia Commons. https://commons.wikimedia.org/wiki/File:Jean_Baptiste_soprano_trombone_(white_bg).png*

    b. **Sopranino Trombone**: If you thought you heard high notes on the soprano trombone, then get ready to hear even higher notes from the sopranino. It is even tinier than the sopranino and the most rare type of trombone to be seen.

    c. **Alto Trombone**: The tenor trombone is like the direct elder sibling of the soprano and sopranino trombones. It has a more elegant tone and is popular in orchestras and chamber music bands. Composers like the legendary Ludwig Beethoven loved using the alto trombone because it blends well with other brass instruments.

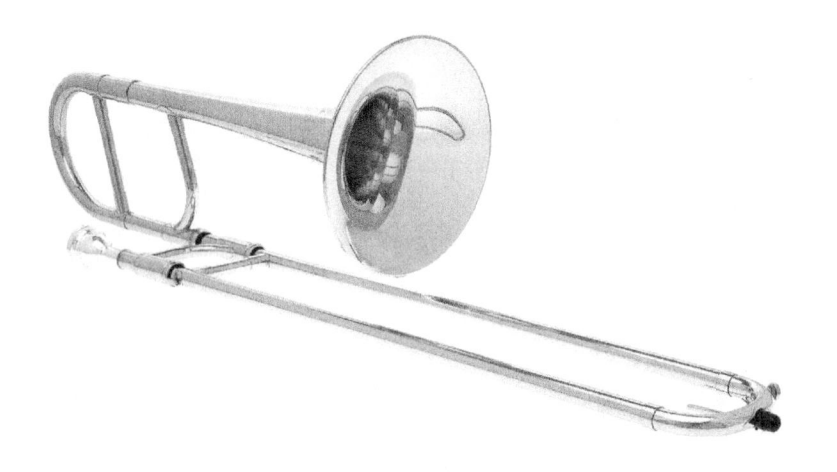

6. *Alto trombone. Source: EnricRllorens, CC BY-SA 4.0 <https://creativecommons.org/licenses/by-sa/4.0>, via Wikimedia Commons.*
https://commons.wikimedia.org/wiki/File:Tromb%C3%B3_alt.jpg

   d. **Tenor Trombone**: This is the most popular type of trombone. It can be used in many different styles of music and is a great place for you to start as a beginner. It also has two types: the straight tenor trombone and the F-attachment tenor. Both are good choices for beginners to learn the trombone from scratch.

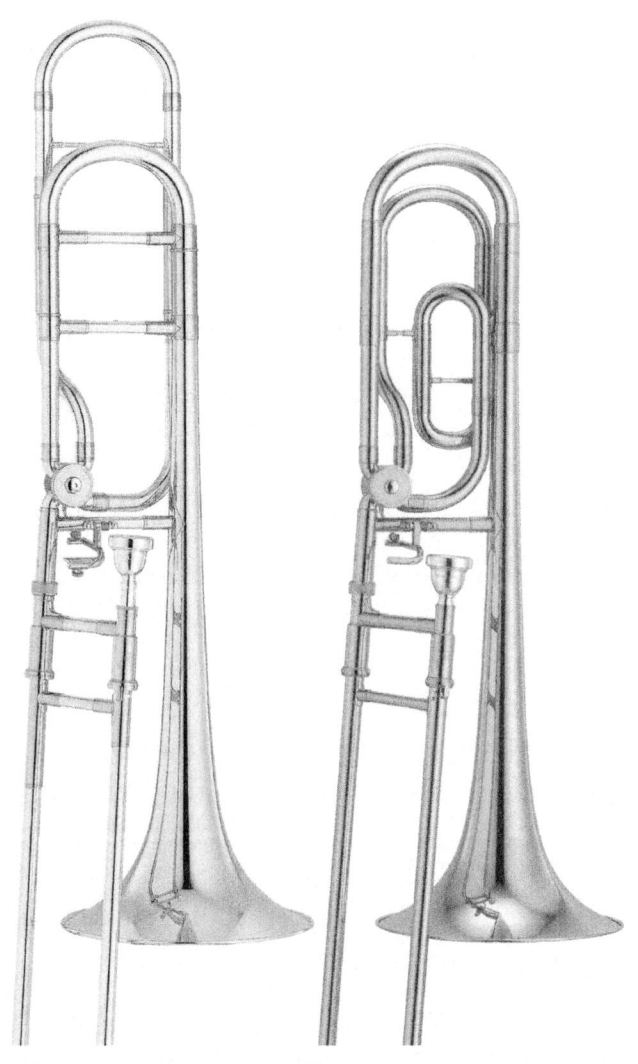

7. *Tenor valve trombone. Source: Collage: Samiclaus, Source images: Yamaha Corporation, CC BY-SA 4.0 <https://creativecommons.org/licenses/by-sa/4.0>, via Wikimedia Commons. https://commons.wikimedia.org/wiki/File:Yamaha_Trombone_comparison_of_open_and_traditional_wrap.jpg*

    e. **Bass Trombone**: The bass trombone is the largest of the trombone family. You can call it the heavyweight champion. It provides a deep, powerful sound that is a foundation for musical pieces in orchestras, brass bands, and jazz bands. The bass trombone has a bigger bore, allowing it to make deep and rumbling sounds.

8. *Bass trombone in E-Flat. Source: Metropolitan Museum of Art, CC0, via Wikimedia Commons.*
https://commons.wikimedia.org/wiki/File:Bass_Valve_Trombone _in_E-flat_MET_211788.jpg

2. **What is the size and range of the trombone?** The size of the trombone affects how easy it is to play, and the kind of sounds it makes. This means a smaller bore size, which is the hole running through the instrument, will produce a high-pitched tone. Bigger trombones sound deeper and richer, but they take more practice and lung power to play. The best size depends on what kind of music you want to play.

3. **What material was used to construct the trombone?** Trombones are made from different materials. They can be made from brass, nickel, or even silver, and each kind makes the trombone sound a bit different. Brass is the most popular choice because it creates a warm, mellow sound. How the trombone is put together, like how smooth the slide is and what kind of finish it has, also affects how long it will last and how it sounds.

4. **The brand and sound quality.** Choose a trombone from a reputable brand. They are known for making high-quality instruments that will last. Sure, a fancy brand might cost more, but they use better materials and ensure the trombone is put together well. This means it will sound better and be easier to play for a longer time. So, while a cheaper trombone might be tempting, a good brand is a better investment in the long run.

5. **What is your budget?** Your budget will play a big role in your choice. You want to pick a trombone that can fit your wallet, too. They come in all sorts of prices, from beginner-friendly to really expensive. The trick is finding one that's good quality without breaking the bank.

Selecting the Right Equipment

When you get a trombone, you'll also need some accessories. These include:

1. **Mouthpiece**: The mouthpiece is like the part of the trombone you blow into. You want to pick a mouthpiece that feels good and gives you good sound. You can get more than one if you wish. It's good to try a few and see which one works best for you.

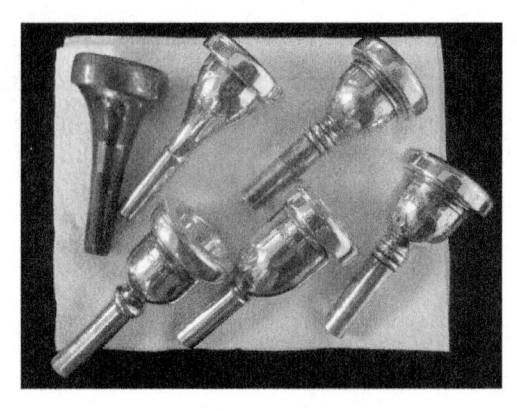

9. *Trombone mouthpieces. Source: Infrogmation of New Orleans, CC BY 2.0 <https://creativecommons.org/licenses/by/2.0>, via Wikimedia Commons. https://commons.wikimedia.org/wiki/File:Trombone_mouthpieces_2.jpg*

2. **Case**: A case is a special box or bag to keep your trombone safe when you're not using it. With a case, you can carry it around more easily. It also helps to prevent your trombone from getting damaged or scratched.

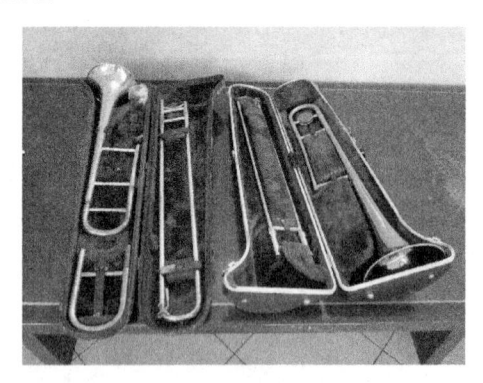

10. *Trombone cases. Source: Infrogmation of New Orleans, CC BY-SA 2.0 <https://creativecommons.org/licenses/by-sa/2.0>, via Wikimedia Commons. https://commons.wikimedia.org/wiki/File:Trombone_cases_2.JPG*

3. **Mute**: A mute is a small device you can put in your trombone to change the sound. It makes the sound softer or different.

11. *Trombone mute. Source: Petra Klawikowski, CC BY-SA 3.0 <https://creativecommons.org/licenses/by-sa/3.0>, via Wikimedia Commons.*
https://commons.wikimedia.org/wiki/File:Posaune_mit_Straight_Mute_KSG_0058_PK.jpg

4. **Trombone Stand**: You don't always have to carry your trombone around; that's what trombone stands are made for. You can put it on the stand, and it will stay in one place. It's good when you need to take a break or if you're playing in a band and must put your trombone down for a bit.

*12. Trombone stand. Source:
https://www.flickr.com/photos/kevglobal/11689309504/*

Understanding the Basic Parts of the Trombone

Learning about the trombone's basic parts will help you easily identify and recognize them. Below is a run-through of the different parts:

1. **Tuning Slide**: This is a special slide at the back of the trombone, like a U-bend. You can push it in and pull it out with a gentle touch. This slide is like a fine-tuning knob for the trombone's sound. Pulling it out stretches the tube, making the trombone sound lower. Pushing it in shortens the tube a smidge, making the sound higher.

2. **The Bell**: Similar to a trumpet, the trombone's bell is a cone shape that gets wider at the end. This helps make the sound louder and project it outwards. When you play, the bell sits right over the slide and points forward over your left shoulder.

3. **Slide**: This is the trombone's most famous feature. Unlike most wind instruments, trombones use a slide instead of buttons or valves to change pitch. The tube gets longer when you push the slide out, making the sound lower. Slide it in, and the tube gets shorter, making the sound higher. This slide is special because it's made from some of the thinnest metal you'll find on any instrument, and because of that, it's important to be careful with your trombone and keep it safe in its case when you're not playing.

4. **Backbore**: There is a short tube right behind the mouthpiece called the backbore or sometimes just the bore. This piece connects the mouthpiece to the slide and also plays a role in how the trombone sounds. Big backbores make the trombone sound deeper, which is great for orchestral music. Smaller backbores create brighter, sharper sounds that work well for jazz, pop, and reggae.

5. **Slide Lock**: This handy little device prevents the slide from popping off. It's a small latch that keeps the outer

slide securely in place when you're not playing. This way, you can hold your trombone without worrying about the slide accidentally falling off and getting damaged.

6. **Water Key**: Playing any wind instrument for a while can leave some wetness inside, and trombones are no different. Luckily, they have a built-in solution called the water key, sometimes called the spit valve. This is a small lever near the front of the trombone that opens a hole in the slide. By pressing the lever, you can drain any moisture collected inside the instrument, which keeps the trombone clean and the sound good.

7. **Slide Braces**: They are located near the mouthpiece and help strengthen and stabilize the slide. The braces are divided into two: one near the mouthpiece that grabs onto the inner slide and another further out that holds the outer slide. When you play, your left-hand grips the first brace to steady the trombone, while your right hand slides the outer slide back and forth to hit the right notes.

8. **Mouthpiece**: The mouthpiece is the funnel-shaped part of the trombone where you blow air to make a sound. They come in different sizes and shapes, so you can pick the mouthpiece that fits you best, depending on the music you want to play. Smaller mouthpieces make brighter sounds and are easier to play high notes on.

Proper Hand Positioning and Posture

Proper Hand Position

On your right hand:

- Use only three fingers: thumb, pointer, and middle finger.
- Your middle finger rests lightly on the bottom part of the brace.
- Your pointer finger is placed next to the middle finger.
- Your thumb goes on the other side.
- Avoid making a fist to prevent tension in the arm.

On your left hand:

- Place your thumb along the back part of the tube.
- Keep your left pointer finger pointing up towards the mouthpiece.
- The other three fingers should be wrapped around the instrument between the braces.
- Maintain this position to help support the trombone.

Proper Posture for Playing the Trombone

13. *You can play the trombone sitting or standing but you must use the proper posture. Source: https://www.pexels.com/photo/a-man-in-blue-polo-playing-the-trumpet-12467206/*

You can either play the trombone sitting or standing. While seated, the proper posture is to:

1. Sit towards the edge of the chair.
2. Avoid using the chair's backrest, as it may cause restriction.
3. Keep your shoulders back and relaxed.
4. Imagine a string from the top of your head to the ceiling to align your head, shoulders, and hips.
5. Place your feet flat on the floor with knees at a 90-degree angle.

If you're playing the trombone standing up, the proper posture is to:

1. Stand with feet even and knees slightly bent.
2. Avoid locking the knees, as it may cause tension.

3. Maintain good posture with shoulders back and relaxed.
4. Keep the same hand positions as when seated.

Whether you are standing or sitting to play the trombone:

1. Ensure you hold the trombone in a diagonal "v" position, not straight up and down.
2. Avoid resting the instrument heavily on the left shoulder to prevent neck strain.
3. Relax your body and maintain the alignment of your head to the trombone for efficient playing and breathing.

Chapter 3: Trombone Playing Techniques

Every musical instrument comes with its own set of techniques. The techniques for playing the guitar are different from those for playing the piano, and both are effective in their own way. So, what exactly are techniques? A technique is a method or way of doing something. When it comes to playing music, technique means how you use your body or parts of it to play the instruments; they are special skills you learn to make the instruments sound great. A good technique will help you avoid making jerky sounds or accidentally hitting the wrong notes.

14. *The trombone has certain techniques you need to learn. Source: https://www.pexels.com/photo/a-young-boy-in-purple-shirt-playing-trombone-14855750/*

For instance, string instruments like the dulcimer involve playing techniques such as fingerpicking, fretting, strumming, and hammering. These kinds of techniques are popular in the family of string instruments. There is nothing to finger pick, fret, or strum on wind instruments like the trumpet, the cornet, or the trombone. They are two different families altogether. Picture your best friend's family for a moment; you'll notice that everyone in their family dresses alike somehow, just like you and your family. In the same way, instruments from different families are played using different techniques.

The trombone is an exceptional instrument and should be played with proper skill and technique. Unlike the other brass instruments, the trombone is the only one in the pack that chose to use a slide instead of valves; however, using the slide requires some skills. It doesn't end there. The techniques for playing the trombone also involve breath control. At this point, learning to play the trombone probably feels like it just got serious. Don't worry. This next chapter will help you understand the techniques used to play the trombone as you read on, and in no time, you will be the one teaching other children how it is done.

In the sections lined up next, you will explore some cool trombone-playing techniques, learn some finger placement tricks and skills to make your playing sound great, discover how you can make magical melodies by using some slide techniques and breath control, and learn about how to develop a sense of pitch and tone to help you play your precious trombone with more accuracy and style.

Basic Trombone Slides and Finger Placement

15. There are certain ways to place your fingers on the trombone. Source: https://www.flickr.com/photos/slgc/6101919144

As you have learned, the trombone uses a slide to change pitch, unlike most brass instruments that use buttons or valves. This slide lets you play a wide range of notes, but it takes some practice to get the hang of it. Here's a breakdown of the first six slide positions on the trombone:

- **First Position**: For the first position, the slide is drawn all the way back, making the tubing the longest, like a long, stretched-out hose. Because the tubing is so long, it vibrates slowly, creating the lowest pitches the trombone can play. It produces a deep, rumbling sound and is perfect for starting off a musical piece.

- **Second Position**: For the second position, you have to push the slide out just a little, maybe about the width of your hand. This shortens the tubing, causing the trombone to vibrate faster and slightly higher in pitch than in the first position. The sound bounces back and forth quickly, creating a slightly higher note.

- **Third Position**: The slide is pulled out a bit further than the second position for the third position. This makes the trombone vibrate faster, creating a higher pitch than before. The sound is bouncing back and forth really quickly now, making a noticeably higher note.

- **Fourth Position**: For the fourth position, the slide is exactly halfway out from the first position. When the slide is brought to this middle point, the trombone vibrates even faster than before, creating a higher pitch than in the previous positions. The sound bounces back and forth super-fast at this position, making a high-pitched sound.

- **Fifth Position**: This is not quite as common as the others, but it is very good at hitting specific notes that fall in between the more standard positions. This position requires you to pull the slide almost all the way out. The fifth position causes the tubing to be so short, making it vibrate very quickly, creating notes that are higher than the fourth position but not quite as high as the sixth position. In this position, the sound is bouncing back and forth extremely fast. This creates a very high-pitched note, but reaching it and playing smoothly might initially feel awkward.

- **Sixth Position**: At the sixth position, the slide is fully extended. This makes the tubing the shortest, creating the highest standard notes the trombone can play. The sound is vibrating incredibly fast, producing a very high-pitched sound. The sixth position lets you play some impressive melodies.

Slide positions can be difficult to master because they require a lot of arm extension and good control of the slide. Don't get discouraged. Stay focused; soon, you will develop the strength and coordination to hit those notes comfortably. It takes time and dedication to play these notes consistently and clearly. Be patient, practice regularly, and focus on conquering the basic techniques. Take it one step at a time. You're already the winner.

Trombone Techniques and Breath Control

- **Glissando**: The glissando is a popular technique that the trombone is known for. Start with the slide all the way out. That's the first note, then pull it in smoothly and steadily all the way to the new note, keeping your air blowing strong the whole time. It's almost like making a long, smooth "woo-woo" sound.

- **Trills**: Trombones have three ways to trill, like rapidly switching between two notes. The most common is the lip trill, used up high where the notes are closer together. Here, you have to move your lips and tongue fast with lots of air to make it sound like a quick rattle.

Another way to achieve trills with trombones is with an F attachment valve. Flick the F valve trigger up and down really fast for a trill, which is especially good for higher notes. Valve trombones can also trill using their valves, just like other instruments.

- **The Flatter**: This one's a bit tricky to explain, but imagine the sound of an airplane taking off. Normally, trombone air flows freely. For flatter, make an "r" sound with your tongue while you blow. It takes practice, but it's a great effect.

- **Tonguing Techniques**: Sometimes, music moves too fast for your regular "ta-ta" tonguing. The best tonguing techniques to use here would be double and triple tonguing. For double tonguing, say "ta-ka" instead – use two different parts of your tongue for each note, making it faster. Triple tonguing is similar, but use three quick tongue motions to say "ta-ta-ka" for triplets.

- **Buzzing**: This might sound funny, but buzzing is serious. Make a wide smile and blow air through your lips like a bee buzzing. This wakes up your facial muscles for playing and gets you ready to go. You can also buzz into the mouthpiece to warm up even more, but remember, let the air do the work, not your muscles.

- **Long Tones**: Grab your trombone and play long, smooth notes after buzzing. Focus on making a nice sound and feeling comfortable, not getting tired. Rest after each note. This helps you play for longer and sound even better.

Breath Control

Did you know that even though we use our bodies for everything, they weren't exactly built to play the trombone? That's especially true when it comes to breathing. Unlike talking or running, playing the trombone needs a special breath, a steady flow of air that keeps your lips buzzing just right. You have to use your whole lungs, not just the shallow part you use for everyday things. Here are some tips to help you understand how your lungs work in different parts:

- **Belly Breath**: Lie comfortably on your back and breathe slowly. Put your hand on your belly and feel it rise and fall as the air fills the bottom part of your lungs.

- **Mid-Breath**: Sit up tall and breathe in again, but keep your shoulders relaxed this time. Notice how your chest expands a little, but your shoulders stay put? This is the middle section of your lungs filling up.

- **Top Breath**: Stand up straight and take a big breath in. As you breathe in this time, slowly raise your arms over your head. Feel that stretch in your upper chest? That's the top part of your lungs getting some air.

With a little practice, you can combine all these breaths into one big, powerful inhale that fills your lungs. This is the kind of breath you want for playing the trombone. There are even special breathing exercises that trombone players use to train their lungs and get even better at this full-body breathing. These exercises help to make your lungs stronger and more efficient. Some famous ones include:

- Inhale for 4 counts, exhale for 8 or 16 counts.

- Inhale for 2 counts, exhale for 4, 8, or 16 counts.

- Inhale for 1 count, exhale for 4, 8, or 16 counts.

As you improve, you can try more challenging exercises, like inhaling for 4 counts and exhaling for 32 counts. When doing these exercises, pay attention to where your breath goes. When you inhale, focus on expanding your belly, not your chest or shoulders. You can even place a hand on your belly to help. Try blowing the air through your mouthpiece. This way, you'll notice your breathing and improve your control.

Daily breathing exercises will help you build your breathing muscles slowly and steadily, just like any other muscle in your body. Training your lungs and learning to take full, deep breaths will ensure you have all the air you need to make beautiful music.

Developing a Sense of Pitch and Tone

Life would be so boring without sounds. Not just music but every other sound in nature. Music is full of exciting sounds, but not all sounds are created equally. Two important factors influence how these sounds are perceived. They are pitch and tone. Pitch can be described as the altitude of a sound. High-pitched sounds are like mountain peaks, while low-pitched sounds are down in the valleys. It all depends on how fast the sound wave vibrates. Faster vibrations create higher pitches, and slower vibrations create lower pitches.

16. Use your voice to figure out the right pitch and tone when you play the trombone. Source: https://unsplash.com/photos/girl-in-blue-and-white-tank-top-IXiGMtCrQPg

Tone adds color to the sound. Each color has a unique quality, just like musical tones. Think of it this way: tone describes the character of a sound. It makes a flute sound different from a violin, even if they're playing the same note. A trumpet can have a bright, brassy tone, while a clarinet might have a warm, mellow tone.

As a musician, you need to develop a good sense of pitch and tone as you progress. You should have these two important elements on your side when playing your trombone. Here are some tips to help you develop this skill:

- Practice singing along with your voice. Use a digital tuner to set a target note and then try to sing that note back. The tuner will let you know if you're hitting the right pitch. This will help train your ear to recognize pitch accurately.

- Actively listen to music and focus on identifying the pitch and tone used. Active listening is like wearing noise-canceling headphones so you can't hear any unwanted noise. Your focus is solely on the music you're trying to play. Train your ear to recognize the changes in pitch and tone, and try to imitate that in your own playing.

- Download ear training apps designed specifically for musicians, such as the ones mentioned in the second article. These apps are packed with lots of exercises and drills to help you develop your sense of pitch and tone through some practice routines.

- Try playing by the ear. Practice playing simple melodies or tunes by ear without relying on sheet music or tabs. Use your ear to guide you in finding the correct pitches and tones on your trombone, and gradually start playing tougher musical pieces, making sure to play by ear.

- Look for materials on how pitch and tone work. Learn about the various pitch techniques, such as pitch bends, slides, vibrato, and tremolo, and how they are used in music. Then, practice them.

Chapter 4: Building Trombone Skills

It's time to get your trombone groove on. Put on your favorite trombone-playing gear and get ready to make some big trombone sounds. Take a deep breath, keep an open mind, and open your ears. You can do anything you put your mind to. Remember, those famous stars who make playing the trombone or any musical instrument look easy didn't just wake up one day playing like that. It takes practice, dedication, and more practice to play like them. It might not be easy initially, but you will surely succeed as you stay focused. Keep going champ.

17. Never stop practicing your trombone skills. Source: https://www.flickr.com/photos/2cheap2keep/53536366754/

Musical scales are one of the key elements of music as an art. You cannot learn to play any musical instrument and not pay attention to scales. This chapter will teach you all you need to know about scales. You only get to play cool songs because of the scales. They're the key to unlocking amazing melodies on musical instruments, and the trombone is not left behind in the business of scales. You will also learn about trombone sheet music and notes. When you think of sheet music, think of those lines and dots that make up the language of tunes. You'll find out how to read music like a pro. Sheet music might seem strange at first, but as you use this guide, those lines will turn into familiar tunes, and you'll speak the music language fluently.

Every slide move and lip trick you master is a step forward in leveling up your trombone skills. Like collecting points in games, every sweet melody you play is a shiny achievement on your musical journey. Get ready to be the boss of tunes in the music game using your trombone. This part might make you work a bit, but the tunes you'll play soon will be super worth it. Time to step up your trombone game and get those musical muscles growing. Give your all to learning scales and trust that you can handle them and make them yours. You can do it.

Learning and Practicing Scales and Simple Melodies

What Are Scales?

If you are familiar with the body parts of a fish, you know it's one of those animals with scales. Those glass-like substances grow out of a fish's skin as a protective layer for their bodies. However, this is music class, not biology class. A musical scale is a set of notes that work well together in a melody or harmony. In music, there are different kinds of scales, the most popular being the major and the minor scales. When you understand musical scales and know what notes belong to which scale, you will have no problem creating the kind of music you love.

Practicing Scales

Every musical scale has its unique key in which it's written, and the specific notes of each scale depend on the key it's written in. A scale is a group of notes that go well together, kind of like a mini-song. They can be sung in ascending and descending order using the solfa notation do, re, mi, fa, so, la, ti, do; and Do, ti, la, so, fa, mi, re, do. Solfa notation is how singers use syllables to remember the order of notes in a scale.

What's amazing about scales is how you can rearrange the notes to produce lively rhythms and melodies. The most common scale for beginners is the Major C scale. To create a major scale, a set formula has been designed to help players get the correct notes for each scale. The formula is: whole step, whole step, half step, whole step, whole step, whole step, half step. This could also be represented as Tone, Tone, Semitone, Tone, Tone, Tone, Semitone. A half step or semitone is the shortest distance between two musical notes, while a whole step or tone is simply two semitones or half steps.

Unlike other instruments, the trombone uses the slide to produce notes, so for the trombone, this general formula is translated to slide positions. Remember those? For the notes on the C major scale, the slide positions include:

- **C (1st position)** - Start with your hand holding the slide all the way to the end, closest to you. This is your hand's home position.

- **D (4th position)** - Move your hand out further on the slide, like you're reaching for something further away.
- **E (3rd position)** - Slide your hand back just a short distance, like taking a small step back.
- **F (1st position)** - Bring your hand back to the starting position where you began.
- **G (4th position**) - Reach out further on the slide again, like before.
- **A (2nd position)** - Slide your hand back in a little bit, but not as much as before. Just take a smaller step back.
- **B (4th position)** - Reach out further on the slide again.
- **C (3rd position**) - Finally, slide your hand back a short distance again. This last C will be higher pitched than the one you first played.

The final note of any scale is usually the higher version of the first note.

Playing Simple Melodies

As a beginner, you don't need to jump straight into playing orchestra pieces and complicated music. Here are some well-known songs that are perfect for you to start with:

- "Amazing Grace" by Traditional
- "All of Me" by John Legend
- Happy Birthday song
- "Happy" by Pharell Williams

Understanding Trombone Sheet Music and Notation

Some people can play music just by listening. But to be even better, you should also learn to read sheet music. That way, you can learn songs faster. You don't need to hear a song before playing it if you can read its notes. There's lots of sheet music online for different kinds of music. And if you want to play with a group, like an orchestra, you must know how to read music because orchestras don't play by ear. So, learning to read music is important if you want to have fun playing with others.

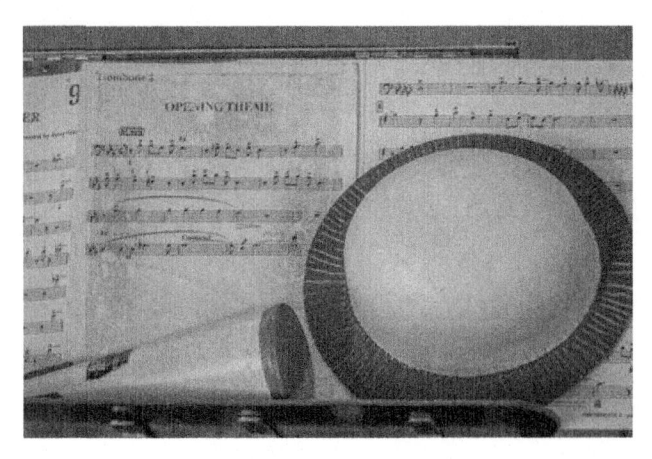

18. Sometimes you need to use sheet music to play a song you like. Source: https://www.flickr.com/photos/sniegowski/51844248941/

The Staff: When you look at sheet music, you'll see something called the staff. It has five lines and four spaces. Each line and space has a note, but you won't know which note unless you know what key the music is in.

- **The Clef**: There is also something called the clef, which shows the musical key. There are two main kinds: treble and bass. The treble looks like a fancy letter "g," and the bass looks like a backward "c" with dots. The notes on the lines and spaces depend on the clef.

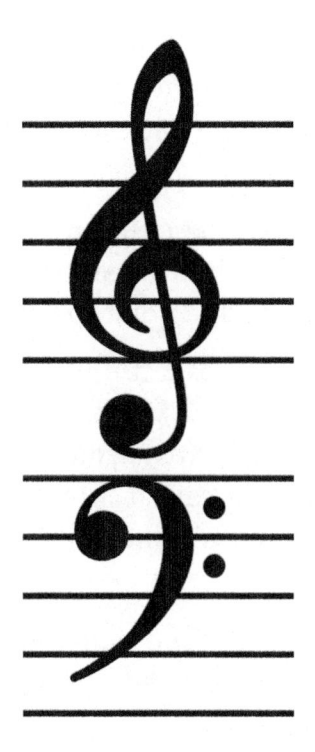

19. The treble and bass clef. Source: G, CC BY-SA 4.0 <https://creativecommons.org/licenses/by-sa/4.0>, via Wikimedia Commons. https://commons.wikimedia.org/wiki/File:Treble_clef_and_Bass_clef.svg

- **The Notes**: The notes in music are represented by English alphabets A to G. On a musical instrument, they are played from A to G, and then you start all over again at A. When written in sheet music, notes themselves can look a little different. Some are circles that are colored in, some are empty circles, and some even have a little line drawn through them. Each note has three parts:

- o **The Head**: This is like the note's face. It can be colored in or empty and sits on a line or space on the ladder, telling you which note to play.
- o **The Stem**: This is like a little tail sticking out from the head, pointing either up or down. Don't worry, which way it points doesn't change the sound, but it helps you read the notes faster.
- o **The Flag**: This is a fun little curvy line you might see next to the tail sometimes. It tells you how long to hold the note. No flag means you hold it for a long time, one flag means a shorter time, and even more flags mean an even shorter time.

- **Key Signatures**: Key signatures show which notes are sharp or flat. They go right after the clef and change depending on the scale you're playing. You won't need any key signatures when playing sheet music that has been written in the key of C major.

- **Time Signatures**: These show the rhythm of the music. They look like fractions and tell you how many beats are in each bar and how long each beat lasts. The most common time signature in musical pieces is 4/4, also called common time. Music has to be set to a rhythm for it to work. Time signatures are usually written at the start of the music staff.

- **Bar Lines**: Bar lines divide the music into bars or measures, like chapters in a book. Each bar has a certain number of beats.

- **Ledger Lines**: If there are too many notes for just the five lines and four spaces, you'll see ledger lines. These extra lines help show higher or lower notes that don't fit on the staff.

Tips for Effective Practice and Developing a Practice Routine

You wouldn't spend all this time learning the trombone if you just wanted to sound groggy, would you? Nobody picks up a trombone, thinking, "I just want it because it looks cute in my arms." You want to make that trombone sing like it could win a Grammy on its own, right? The key to unlocking trombone greatness is consistent practice, but not just any practice. This means focused sessions that will take your playing to the next level. With these tips, you'll practice your trombone more often and see much faster improvement.

1. Pick exactly what you want to improve on. Is it mastering a tricky part of your favorite song or learning a new method? Set goals that challenge you but are still realistic. Don't rush yourself. Break down big goals into smaller, achievable steps. Make sure your goals fit your overall musical dreams. Do you want to join a band? Focus on learning the music bands play. Are you hoping to impress friends and family? Pick a song you know they'll love. Set deadlines to stay on track. Give yourself a month to learn a new section of a song, or aim to practice a specific technique for 15 minutes a day for a week.

2. Instead of just messing around, build a practice plan that focuses on specific skills like how to hold the mouthpiece for a good sound, how fast and smooth

your fingers move, controlling your breathing for better tone, and learning pieces from different types of music to expand your musical horizon.

3. Never jump straight into playing. First, spend some time doing a proper warm-up. Make that part of your routine. For example, it could be playing the C major scale in ascending and descending order to get your lips and lungs ready.

4. Don't try to do everything at once. When learning a song, take it step-by-step: first, learn the notes themselves, then focus on playing them with the right rhythm and timing, and finally, add feeling and expression after you understand the basics. If you practice too much, you might burn out. Take breaks sometimes to keep yourself motivated and avoid injuries or strain.

5. You know how you always brush your teeth before bed, right? It's like a habit now. Your practice time can also become a habit if you let it. Practice becomes easier with a routine. You can schedule your practice session to come right before something you do daily; that way, it soon becomes a natural habit.

6. Recording yourself play is also a great tool to track progress and identify the areas your playing still sounds funny. Anytime you're feeling discouraged, you can listen to the previous recordings you made and be amazed at how far you've come. They will also help pinpoint your weaknesses so you know what to focus on in future sessions.

7. Pick a spot where you can confidently blow your trombone without worrying about who is listening or if

you're disturbing the neighborhood. Find somewhere that you can play with the most focus.

Chapter 5: Playing Trombone Music

Imagine your parents had a bakery that offered every cake flavor ever imagined. That would be awesome, right? Each time you enter this bakery, it's like entering a world of sweetness and delight, with rows upon rows of cakes in every flavor. Now, think about this: why limit yourself to just one type of cake? Sure, you might have a favorite, but there's a whole universe of flavors waiting to be explored, and you could be the one humming with delight at how the cakes melt in your mouth and rubbing your belly.

20. There are so many options when it comes to picking the music you play with the trombone. Source: https://unsplash.com/photos/musical-notes-on-music-sheet-stand-KMbIBPBwm28

You could try bold combinations like chocolate, orange, vanilla, and lavender. Most of these combinations might sound unusual at first, but you'll never know how delicious they can be until you taste them. If you are willing to try new things, you might stumble upon unique flavor combinations nobody has ever experienced.

Think about this in music. If you only ever listen to one style of music, you might start to feel bored after a while. It's like eating the same type of cake every day — it's nice, but it can get boring. However, if you open yourself up to different styles and genres worldwide, you'll be amazed at what you discover. Before you know it, you might be inspired to mix different styles and develop an original genre that isn't in any music theory book yet.

This whole chapter is about why stepping outside your comfort zone and exploring different types of music is so important. It's an adventure, just like trying out a crazy new cake flavor. The musical journey that awaits you is just as sweet and satisfying as that perfect slice of your favorite cake, maybe even more so because of all the amazing discoveries you'll make along the way. You will also learn some new styles to improve your trombone skills. Are you ready for this next phase?

Exploring Different Musical Genres and Styles

The world is always changing, and that's also true for music. If you're a musician and only listen to the same kind of music all the time, you're missing out on all the new and exciting sounds being created. Nowadays, it's important to be open-minded and listen to different types of music.

Are you ready to explore some new sounds? It's time to take a look at a few different music genres you might not be familiar with. Break away from that playlist you've been listening to on repeat and discover something new.

- **Jazz Music**: Jazz is another genre of music where the trombone is a star player. Back in the early days of jazz, trombone players were like the backbone of the music band. They used the slide on their trombone to play sounds that were almost like someone talking through a megaphone. This helped develop jazz's unique "tailgate" style, where the music felt lively and exciting. But jazz kept changing and growing, and so did the way the trombone was used. Some famous trombone players in this era, like Tommy Dorsey and J.J. Johnson, were known for their incredible skill and ability to play the trombone in brass bands.

- **Classic Music**: The trombone is like one of the best actors in classical music. It can play different roles. It sometimes delivers soft and mellow tones, which blend well with the other instruments. The trombone can also produce a loud and majestic sound, perfect for grand moments in the music. Musicians from the Romantic era took centerstage with their trombones carrying melodies from their hearts straight into the ears of their listeners. Composers like Wagner and Mahler appreciated the trombone's flexibility. They took advantage of the trombone's wide range of notes; with it, they could evoke lots of emotions through their music.

- **Pop Music**: Trombones aren't the stars of today's pop and most new music, that's for sure. That doesn't mean they don't get to join the party sometimes. Think of a pop song you like, and then imagine that same song with a trombone popping in now and then. It will certainly make the whole thing even more interesting. That's what the trombone can do in pop music. It breaks things up a bit from the usual sounds and adds a bright, brassy voice that can be strong and exciting, just like the music itself. Bands like Chicago and James Brown thought so, too, and they used trombones in their music to give it an extra burst of energy.

- **Ska Music**: In a music style with a happy, upbeat vibe like ska, the trombone is usually heard hanging out with the instruments in the "horn section." This section specializes in playing short, exciting bursts of sound that produce beautiful melodies. The trombone players can play the notes in a way in which they don't quite land on the beat but are kind of in-between. This offbeat style adds an unexpected vibe to the music and makes you want to move your body even more!

- **Reggae Music**: The trombone can also add smooth and mellow tones to reggae music with a more relaxed feel. It can play long, flowing notes, creating a calming and peaceful atmosphere. It is a versatile instrument, so there is room for it in almost all kinds of music.

- **Salsa**: Trombones are perfect for salsa music. They fit right in with the happy, upbeat rhythms and add strong melodies that make you want to move. Salsa players get to show off with short, fun melodies during the montuno part. The trombone's slide lets them bend notes beautifully in fast and clean playing, with both smooth and bouncy styles. Trombones never fail to keep the party lively and fun for everyone.

Techniques for Expressive and Emotive Playing

If you can play a simple melody like the "Happy Birthday" song on your trombone, that's awesome. However, if you give that same song to a professional trombone player, someone who plays for a living, they can take that same simple song and make you feel all kinds of things. They might play it slow and quiet, making you feel sad or peaceful. Or maybe they play it loud and strong, like a band of soldier musicians, making you feel excited. That style of playing that makes you feel emotions is called expressive and emotive playing. Professional players know how to change how loud or soft they play a note, which can make a huge difference. They use special techniques to make this happen. Here are some of them:

1. **Staccato**: Playing staccato on the trombone needs to be precise. Staccato means playing short, not accenting the note. Your tongue and lips need to work together well to get it right. Sometimes, beginners try to do too much with their tongue, but often, the problem lies with the embouchure – how your lips are set. The note won't come out right if your lips don't start vibrating when they should. So, practice making a "ha" sound with a little force. Once your embouchure is set for a note, it should respond with less effort. Make sure your tongue makes a clean seal to end the note. Some players use their tongue to stop the note with a "tut" sound or to prepare for the next note, but this can mess up your staccato. Instead, use "tuh" or "teh" sounds for cleaner staccato. Your throat should close quickly after you start the note, and a slight decrease in volume is natural. To sum up, staccato needs precise production, good breath support, and quick throat closure. Practicing with a "ha" articulation can help.
2. **Legato**: Playing legato on the trombone can be just as expressive as on other instruments. It's not easy, but with practice, it can sound effortless. The key to good legato is keeping a continuous air flow and making the notes blend smoothly. There are different ways you can do this:
    a. Using natural slurs. This involves moving the slide opposite the notes, legato-tonguing, and even playing without tonguing. Natural slurs are the smoothest, where you change notes without moving the slide. Practicing slurs helps control the complex muscles needed for legato.

b. Moving the slide opposite the notes is another method, especially for higher notes. Legato-tonguing uses the tongue to help place notes but keeps the air flowing. You can use different syllables like "thee," "thoo," or "lee" to find what works best. Tongue-less legato is possible at lower volumes but needs good control. So, you can play a beautiful legato in many ways, each with its own benefits.

3. **The Pause**: Taking a break in your music, called a pause, can make it feel more emotional. When you're playing, try to find places to stop for a moment. Music with pauses can feel even more emotional because those pauses are like taking a deep breath before something important. They give the listener a chance to really listen and soak in what you've just played, making the next part of the music sound even stronger.

4. **Vibrato**: A controlled vibrato will make your trombone-playing sound. There are different ways to produce vibrato, but some are better than others. Slide vibrato is common in jazz but has limitations. Diaphragm vibrato mimics vocal techniques and adds a singing quality to your playing. Lip vibrato is smoother and closer to slide vibrato but needs good control. Throat and head vibrato are less common and not recommended. Depending on your style of music, you might focus on one type of vibrato over another. Band players might use diaphragm vibrato, while symphonic players need a range of vibrato techniques.

5. **Dynamics**: You can play loudly or softly to make your trombone playing sound more interesting. That's not all, though; you also add small changes in volume to make the music more alive. For example, making the

sound gradually louder or softer can add a lot of feeling to the music. To get good at this, you must practice controlling your breath and changing the volume smoothly daily. You can practice getting gradually louder and softer and changing suddenly from loud to soft. Doing this will help you improve, and you'll find it easier in harder songs later.

Chapter 6: Trombone Care and Maintenance

Now that you've learned how to play the trombone, you must take care of it so it can last a long time and work as best as possible. The trombone is an exceptional musical instrument, but it's also really delicate. This means you should look after it carefully. You wouldn't wear a set of clothes for a week without washing them, would you? Before wearing them again, you wash those clothes to take care of them. The same goes for your precious trombone.

21. It's important to always take care of your trombone. Source: https://www.flickr.com/photos/slgc/5678154341

You must take care of your trombone so it stays in good shape for a long time. After you play, spend a little time cleaning it to stop water and dirt from building up, which could make it rusty and damaged. You want your trombone to always look shiny and new. How you store and handle your trombone is also important. If you are not using it, make sure you keep it safe from potential accidents. Don't worry; you will learn all about how to take care of your trombone in this chapter.

Despite your best efforts, there are some common issues that you will encounter with your trombone from time to time. For instance, if the slide gets stuck and refuses to move, it can be frustrating, but knowing how to fix these problems can save you time and money. You will also learn tips and tricks to help you with those as you read.

Taking the time to care for your instrument shows that you are committed to your musical career and respect your trombone. Always show it some love.

How to Keep Your Trombone in Top Condition

Keeping your trombone in great shape is not a hard task. It's way easier than you might think. It can even make you feel proud of yourself for taking care of something you love. It would be awesome to know your trombone sounds perfect every time you pick it up, wouldn't it? Plus, it will still look shiny and new long after you have become best friends with it. So, are you ready to learn what it takes to keep your trombone in top condition? Just follow these simple steps:

1. **Clean the Mouthpiece**: You use a special brush to clean the inside of the mouthpiece at least once a week.

This gets rid of any leftover food bits. Use warm water and a little soap (like dish soap) to wash the mouthpiece inside and out. You can use a soft cloth for the outside. Rinse the mouthpiece with clean water and dry it completely before using it again.

2. **Keep the Slide Smooth**: If your slide feels slow or rough, it needs some oil to make it move smoothly again. Take the slide apart carefully. There should be a little latch you need to open. Put a few drops of slide oil on the inside of the slide where the metal touches. You don't need a lot! Put the slide back together and wipe off any extra oil.

3. **Deeply Clean the Trombone**: Give your trombone a deep clean once a month. Fill a bathtub with warm, soapy water and take your trombone apart (carefully!). Use a special long brush called a snake to clean the inside of the tubes. Rinse everything with clean water and dry it completely before putting it back together.

4. **Swabbing the Inside**: You can also use a cleaning rod and a small cloth to clean the inside of the tubes. Wrap the cloth around the end of the rod and put it inside the tubes. Wipe away any moisture and slide oil inside before putting your trombone back together.

5. **Clean the Body of the Trombone**: Every day, you can wipe down the outside of your trombone with a soft cloth to remove fingerprints or smudges. This helps keep it looking nice and protects the finish.

Storage and Handling Guidelines

- Get a strong case for your trombone to keep it safe and clean. When you're done playing, make sure the round part (the bell) sits properly in the case. Put the slide in carefully so it doesn't bump into anything. Ensure you close the case all the way so the soft lining holds your trombone snugly.

- Just like you wash your hands before eating, you should wash your hands before playing your trombone. Food bits left behind can make your trombone sound funny and smell not-so-great.

- If you wash your trombone, make sure it's completely dry before putting it away.

- Too much moisture is not good for your trombone, plastic, or metal, and it can make it sound weird. So, find a dry place for your trombone to rest when you're not playing, like on a music stand.

- Do not leave your trombone outside on a hot day or while the weather is freezing. If it's hot, find a cool spot for it. If it's chilly, keep it indoors.

Troubleshooting Common Issues

Identifying and addressing the common trombone slide issues helps the quality of the instrument's performance for a long time. Regularly cleaning and inspecting your instrument can prevent many problems, while professional repair may be necessary for more severe issues. One of the most important parts of your trombone is the slide. It allows you to change notes smoothly and precisely. However, like any other part of the instrument, the slide can run into some problems, making playing difficult. Here's a breakdown of some common issues and how to identify them:

The Slide and Dirt Buildup

The most common problem trombone slides face is dirt buildup. Imagine trying to slide smoothly on a dusty floor – that's what happens when dirt and grime get stuck on your slide. Even if you use slide oil, which helps things move smoothly, it won't work as well if there's a layer of dirt underneath. That's why it's important to clean your slide regularly. You can do this with a special cleaning rod and some gentle cleaning chemicals.

There Is a Dent or Ding on Your Slide

Sometimes, your slide might get bumped or hit, leaving a dent. These dents are like little bumps in the road for your slide, making it stick in certain spots and preventing smooth movement. You can usually check for dents by looking closely at the slide or by running your fingers along its length to feel for any unevenness. If you find a dent, it's best to take your trombone to a professional repair person. They have the tools and skills to fix the dent and get your slide sliding smoothly again.

Your Slide Is Bending Out of Shape

You might be surprised to learn that trombone slides can actually bend. This can happen from accidents or even just from normal use over time. A bent slide can cause all sorts of problems, just like a bent straw makes it hard to drink. Hold your slide to a bright light to see if it is bent. Look for the lines that run along the length of the slide. If those lines aren't perfectly straight, even slightly off, your slide is bent. Simply take your trombone to a professional who can straighten it out and ensure it's back in top playing condition.

Watch for these common problems, and take good care of your trombone as much as you can so it continues to sound its best.

Chapter 7: Exploring Trombone History and Repertoire

You made it to the last chapter. You should be proud of yourself for coming this far. It's time to learn about how your new best friend came into existence. The trombone did not just fall from the sky. Like every other musical instrument, it has a history. So, buckle up because you're about to travel through time and learn all about it. Just picture yourself stepping into a time machine, zooming back hundreds of years. You might see people playing trombones in grand churches or even at royal palaces. The trombone was played everywhere. Its deep sound would fill the air during important ceremonies and celebrations.

22. There are many famous trombone players around the world.
Source: https://www.flickr.com/photos/rockvocals/6934797185

Next, you will discover some of the most famous trombone players ever. These people truly showed the world how amazing the trombone could be. They played it with such skill that audiences were blown away, and they even helped write new music specifically for the trombone; their music helped to highlight just how many different sounds and emotions a single trombone could create. This chapter will introduce you to all these famous stars, and you can learn something from their stories and playing styles.

Fast forward to today, lots of musicians are still finding new ways to play it today. Some are using technology to change the sound of the trombone, while others are playing it with musicians from all sorts of different music styles. Before this chapter wraps up, you will also explore the modern development and innovations of the trombone. No matter how they play it, the trombone remains a fun and exciting instrument that can make all kinds of music. Get ready to be inspired by the timeless charm of the trombone.

The Culture and History of the Trombone

Long ago, back in the 14th century, there was a slide trumpet. It was like a trumpet, but it had this special slide thingy that let musicians change the notes they played. People used to play it at fancy parties and stuff in medieval Europe, along with other windy instruments like shawms. These parties must have been pretty cool with all those tooty instruments. Then, around the 15th century, the slide trumpet was upgraded and turned into what we know today as the trombone. Somebody added an extra slide, making it easier for musicians to change notes without doing crazy movements. This made the trombone super popular in Italy, Germany, and other places during the 16th and 17th centuries. People couldn't get enough of it, especially in churches and fancy music groups.

In the late 1600s, things started to slow down for the trombone. People were more into stringy music than windy ones, so the trombone had a bit of a rough patch. But it made a comeback in the 18th century, especially in places like Vienna, where they were all about holy music and fancy operas. Famous composers like Mozart thought the trombone was pretty cool and used it a lot in their music. Ever since then, the trombone has become more popular among music bands and orchestras. By the 20th century, jazz musicians started playing the trombone too. Now you can hear trombones in all kinds of music.

Famous Trombone Players and Important Trombone Compositions

Around the middle of the 1920s, big bands started having not just one but a bunch of trombone players together. This made way for the first trombone player to stand out and do solos. However, the trombone didn't get as much love and attention as it deserved. Some people still considered it a backup for other musicians, but it's way more than that.

You may have seen lots of trombones around, but you may not know the people who play them. Trombone music is everywhere, from big bands to fancy concerts. Here are some famous trombone players you should know about:

- **James Louis Johnson**: J.J. Johnson was one of the biggest jazz players after World War II. He practiced every day to get better at his craft. People call him a jazz legend because he changed the way people play the trombone forever, especially in a kind of music called bebop. Bebop is fast and exciting, and J.J. Johnson could play the trombone just as fast as the saxophone and trumpet players. He was nicknamed "the Charlie Parker of the trombone" because he was so good. J.J. Johnson wasn't just a fast player; his music was excellent, too. He remains an inspiration to trombone players worldwide.

- **Wycliffe Gordon**: Gordon is a great trombone player who likes to try new things. He is one of the few players who plays the trombone in all sorts of ways. He could make the trombone sound like he was singing through it. Wycliffe Gordon is also a singer and songwriter. With his creativity, he keeps pushing the boundaries of what a trombone can do, playing jazz, classical, and gospel tunes.

23. Wycliffe Gordon. Source: The United States Army Band, CC BY 2.0 <https://creativecommons.org/licenses/by/2.0>, via Wikimedia Commons.
https://commons.wikimedia.org/wiki/File:Wycliffe_Gordon_playing_euphonium.jpg

- **Urbie Green**: Urbie is a big name in jazz music. If you like music that makes you want to move and groove, listen to Urbie Green play his trombone. He helped change jazz music forever, making it even more exciting and fun. Urbie Green wasn't just any trombone player. He played with some of the biggest music stars, like Frank Sinatra and Ella Fitzgerald. He even had his own band and wrote his own music. Urbie started his trombone playing at 12 years old, lasting for decades.

- **Nick Hudson**: Nick Hudson is a super-talented trombone player from the UK. He wanted to be as good as some famous trombone players and made it happen. Nick Hudson started playing trombone in a special music group called the Salvation Army. After that, he played in a famous band called the Fodens Band, where he was the main trombone player. He's so good that people call him a legend in brass band music.

Modern Developments and Innovations

Modern trombones are made bigger, so they sound even better. Engineers have also added a new part to trombones to play more notes, and that's not all. Trombones can be made of lighter stuff, so they're easier to hold, especially for children. Some trombones are now made with electronics inside them. These electronics can make the trombone sound louder, softer, or even make different sounds.

Musicians around the world are getting more creative with trombones. For instance, they also sing while they play. If you ever want to learn more about the trombone, there is lots of info about it online now, so it's easier to learn how to play one. You can even hear trombones in movies and TV shows. With all these cool changes, the trombone is more exciting and versatile than ever. What's more? It's only going to get better in the future.

Conclusion

Congratulations! You are officially the latest trombone player in town. In the end, playing the trombone is all about joy and creativity. As you've learned throughout this book, the trombone allows you to express yourself through music. Whether you're just starting and learning the very first notes or have been playing for a long time and want to get even better, every single note you play is a step forward in your musical adventure.

Learning the trombone is always worth the effort. Every time you practice, every new song you learn takes you closer to mastering this beautiful instrument. So, if you ever feel frustrated or like giving up, keep going! Every challenge you overcome makes you a stronger musician. As you keep playing your trombone, remember to listen just as much as you play. Pay attention to all the sounds around you, like the music in nature, the songs you love the most, or even the rhythm of everyday life. Inspiration can come from anywhere, and by being open to the world around you, you'll find new and exciting ways to express yourself through your trombone.

Playing the trombone should make you happy and fulfilled. Don't be afraid to experiment, try new things, and let your creativity shine! Whether you're practicing alone in your room or playing for a big crowd, let your love of music guide you and make your playing even better.

Remember, this musical adventure is not a race to the finish line. There will always be new things to learn, new songs to master, and new challenges to overcome. So, enjoy the process, celebrate how far you've come, and never stop trying to be the best trombone player you can be.

As you put this book down and pick up your trombone, remember the power you hold in your hands. You can create beautiful music and touch the hearts of the people around you. So, confidently play with all your passion and let the music take you to amazing places.

References

12 Famous Trombone Players and their Trombone Performance (Great Trombonists) - CMUSE. (2018, January 25). Www.cmuse.org. https://www.cmuse.org/famous-trombone-players/

Alecia, S. (2023, August 30). Trombone Types & Their Unique Characteristics [Upd. 2023]. PrimeSound.org. https://primesound.org/trombone-types/

Anyabuine, J. (2023, January 27). 10 Terrific Facts About The Trombone. The Fact Site. https://www.thefactsite.com/trombone-facts/

Baines, A. C. (n.d.). Trombone History. Www.lysator.liu.se. https://www.lysator.liu.se/~backstrom/trombone.html

Bradly. (2022, May 30). Different Types of Trombones. MusicalHow.com. https://www.musicalhow.com/types-of-trombones/

Buja, M. (2015, July 8). Instruments of the Orchestra XI: The Trombone. Interlude. https://interlude.hk/instruments-orchestra-xi-trombone/

Farrant, D. (2020, March 12). A Brief History of the Trombone | Hello Music Theory. Https://Hellomusictheory.com/. https://hellomusictheory.com/learn/history-of-the-trombone/

Farrant, D. (2021a, February 21). How To Hold A Trombone: A Beginners' Guide To Proper Grip. Hello Music Theory. https://hellomusictheory.com/learn/how-to-hold-trombone/

Farrant, D. (2021b, March 27). The Different Parts of a Trombone | Hello Music Theory. Https://Hellomusictheory.com/. https://hellomusictheory.com/learn/parts-of-the-trombone/

Gee, H. (2021, November 29). 11 Famous Trombone Players. Orchestra Central. https://orchestracentral.com/famous-trombone-players/

Goods, E. (2021, February 17). 4 Tips To Make Your Trombone Play More Expressively. RS Berkeley Musical Instruments. https://www.rsberkeley.com/blog/make-your-trombone-play-more-expressively

Griffin, M. (2021, December 15). Trombone Parts Explained. Orchestra Ensemble. https://orchestraensemble.com/trombone/trombone-parts-explained/

Grifski, J. (2019, September 3). 8 Easy Ways to Get Better at Trombone. Trill Trombone. https://trilltrombone.com/learn/easy-ways-to-get-better-at-trombone/

Grimes, D. (2022, November 20). Top 10 Problems Facing Beginner Trombonists (And How You Can Help!). Houghton Horns. https://houghtonhorns.com/blogs/articles/top-10-problems-for-beginner-trombonists-and-how-you-can-help

How to choose the right trombone. (2022, September 22). Digital School. https://digital-school.net/how-to-choose-the-right-trombone/

How to Play the Trombone: Step by Step for Beginners. (2022, June 1). Brass 'N Wind. https://brassnwind.com/how-to-play-the-trombone/

Kai. (2023, May 31). Trombone Facts. Facts.net. https://facts.net/trombone-facts/

Kayode, L. (2021, April 28). Trombone - The Wind Instrument History & Music. Phamox Music. https://phamoxmusic.com/trombone/

Kennedy, J. (2014, April 23). How to Take Care of Your Trombone – For Beginners of All Ages. The Eighth Position. https://8thposition.wordpress.com/2014/04/23/how-to-take-care-of-your-trombone/

Kleinhammer, E. (1999). The Art of Trombone Playing. Alfred Music.

Larson, A. (2024, February 7). Perfect Posture and Breathing for Trombone | Digitaltrombone. Digital Trombone. https://www.digitaltrombone.com/perfect-posture-and-breathing-for-trombone.html

Mckeown, A. (2013, October 16). Which Trombone is Right for Me? | Normans Blog. Normans Musical Instruments. https://www.normans.co.uk/blogs/blog/choosingatrombone

Nguyethoang. (2023, September 8). Mastering Trombone Slide Positions: A Step-By-Step Guide. Medium. https://medium.com/@nguyethoang435/mastering-trombone-slide-positions-a-step-by-step-guide-7a106f4944c

Schwartz, D. (2014). Proper Trombone Posture for Beginners. Www.youtube.com. https://www.youtube.com/watch?v=2fyQSgpsZ7A

The Trombone. (2014). A & G Central Music. https://www.schoolmusiconline.com/the-trombone

VanderGraaff, Z. (2022, December 2). 29 Best Trombone Players Of All Time (With Video). Dynamic Music Room. https://dynamicmusicroom.com/best-trombone-players/

Whitaker, L. (2024, February 9). What Should I Consider Before I Buy a Trombone? (with picture). WiseGEEK. https://www.wisegeek.net/what-should-i-consider-before-i-buy-a-trombone.htm

Wick, D. (1996). Trombone technique. Music Dept., Oxford University Press.

Wright, A. (2022, January 13). Parts of a Trombone: A Complete Guide to 18 Important Pieces. Swimmers. https://swmrs.com/parts-of-a-trombone/

Printed in Great Britain
by Amazon